NATIONAL GEOGRAPHIC SOCIETY

DESTINATION
POLAR REGIONS

BY JONATHAN GRUPPER

NATIONAL GEOGRAPHIC SOCIETY
WASHINGTON, D.C.

Polar Bear in a Storm

Awoooooh!

January. The wind rushes against you. Your skin stings from the cold. Beads of ice shower down from a sky as black as night can be. All you can think of is, what could possibly live here?

Welcome to the Arctic.

The Earth is capped by two polar regions—the Arctic Ocean, to the north, and the continent of Antarctica, to the south. These are the coldest, windiest, driest, and harshest places on the planet. Temperatures can drop lower than minus 100° Fahrenheit! But believe it or not, there are plenty of animals and plants that call these regions home. The wildlife at each pole is very different, but all have something in common—surviving in their tough habitat. How do they do it?

The ground shakes beneath you. Look there! A polar bear slams against the ice with his front paws. The Arctic ice may be 12 feet thick, but he's found a thin section he can break through to the ocean below. He pulls a ringed seal to the surface—food enough to last him for five days. Now he rolls around, using the snow like a towel to dry himself off!

The polar bear is the perfect animal for the Arctic. Its fur is thick and specially layered to keep it warm. Its feet are padded so it can move quietly and without slipping, to surprise its prey. This bear is strong, fast, and ferocious.

During winter in the Arctic, it's dark almost every hour of the day. In a cozy den dug deep in the snow, a mother tenderly nurses her newborn twins. She goes without eating until the spring. That's when her cubs are finally ready to follow her to the sea and the seals.

Ringed Seal in an Ice Hole

4

Mother Polar Bear with Cubs

Arctic Sea Stars

By May the sun is back and shining strong. But touch the water—it's still cold as an ice cube. You put on a pair of flippers, a heavy rubber suit, and an oxygen tank and dive in!

What could live underwater beneath the ice? Take a look. A colorful reef stretches in every direction. A clam bed, wide as a football field, carpets the seafloor. Strange jellyfish glow in the darkness near sea anemones and starfish, coral and tiny crustaceans. Every creature is designed to cope with the cold. Now their world is in for a surprise, thanks to the sun. The Arctic is about to melt.

Hurry! Your tank is almost out of oxygen. You swim fast to your ice hole and climb back to the surface—just in time. Suddenly you hear a loud *crack*. The ice is breaking up. Great big chunks are ramming against even bigger chunks. For many animals that's good news.

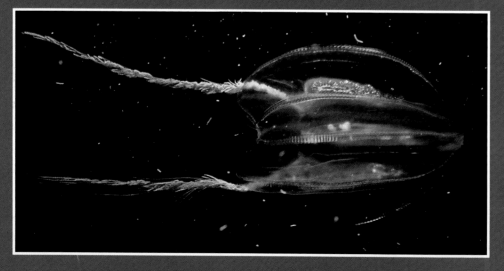

Zooplankton

Ice Diver

Out of the water rises a tusk tall as a man, attached to the head of a beautiful, freckled whale. Have you spotted a unicorn of the sea? No, it's a narwhal. In fact, the melting pack ice has cleared a path for a whole pod of them. Now, with the spring, they're free to swim in where the ice is open and eat.

Beluga and orca, bowhead and gray whales. Some eat cod, some plankton, but for all these ocean giants the Arctic's waters are home. And they're not alone....

Narwhal

Coastal Walrus Colony

The poor walrus! Imagine if the place where you lived melted every year. Soon it will have to leave the ice pans it's used to and swim to a strange new world: the land. At least it won't have to make the trip alone. Walruses do everything together, including fight.

They can weigh more than a ton each, so you'd better stay clear when they jab each other with their three-foot-long tusks. Those are teeth, but walruses don't use them to eat. They use their whiskers to find food! They feel around for clams, then suck the clams out of their shells.

A Tangle of Walrus Tusks

Every day it's getting warmer. Having four inches of fat helps walruses stay cozy in winter. But now it makes them hot and grouchy.

Lazing Walrus

Yes, this is the Arctic too—the land surrounding the ocean, known as the tundra. It's July, and the sun is shining almost every hour of the day and night. Wildflowers that blossom here must grab the short summer while they can.

They're specially designed to make the most of it. Some grow close to the ground where it's warmer. Some have petals that move with the sun as it passes across the sky. Others have a thin layer of hair that keeps them snug.

But this is no time to stop and admire the flowers. The ground is rumbling; 200,000 animals are fast approaching....

Moss Campion

Western Shooting Star

Tundra Rose

Arctic Poppies

Caribou Crossing a River

The air is filled with the sound of thundering hoofs and loud grunts. Wherever you look there's confusion. A great herd of reindeer—also called caribou—is on the move. Every summer they travel hundreds of miles to find food and a place to give birth to their young.

Calves have to learn to walk right away so they can keep up. Staying with the herd is important protection for caribou, and for musk-oxen too. A stray is at risk from one of the Arctic's deadliest predators: the wolf.

Caribou Calf

You hear a lone howl, then other howls rising to meet it. Like white lightning, a pack of wolves descends on a herd of musk-oxen, causing a stampede. In the mad rush, a stray calf loses sight of its mother—and now, with amazing skill and teamwork, the wolves single it out and chase it down.

It may seem cruel, but it's a fight to survive here. The wolves, after all, have their own pups to feed, and there isn't all that much food to go around.

Wolves Hunting Musk-Oxen

Arctic Wolf with Pup

Arctic Wolves on the Move

Hungry? Wherever you find a meal in the Arctic, watch out. You never know who might be dropping by to share a bite....

You turn to face a grizzly bear—at 500 pounds, one of the largest land predators on Earth. Step aside! A pack of gray wolves feasting on a moose calf scatters, leaving their meal for the newcomer.

She has reason to eat well: to fatten up. Already autumn is on its way, and the grizzly will soon be hibernating—sleeping the seasons away for seven long months. But even after she's had her fill, there's still enough meat for yet another appetite. A magnificent golden eagle sweeps in to carry off a portion that weighs as much as he does.

In the Arctic, nothing goes to waste.

Grizzly Bear Mother with Twins in Southern Range

To his cliffside nest far from the reach of predators, the golden eagle delivers his catch to his mate and their two eaglets. By summer's end, birds by the millions have flocked to the Arctic from across the globe.

Look up! Another cliff is covered with thousands of murres, all fishing for cod. How does a creature of the sky catch one of the sea? Murres can swim! They dive-bomb the ocean, staying underwater for up to two minutes.

The ptarmigan is one of the few birds that stays in the Arctic year-round. So its predators can't spot it, it wears white in winter, then changes to brown feathers in summer.

Ptarmigan with Winter Feathers   *Ptarmigan with Summer Feathers*

And then there's the migration champion of the world. To have polar summer weather all the time, the arctic tern travels farther than any other bird. In a few weeks, it will fly 10,000 miles to the other end of the globe—a trip it makes twice a year. Hop on! Let's take a flight of fancy on a tern's back....

Arctic Tern in Flight

Emperor Penguins
with Chick

By the time you arrive in Antarctica, it's November. But while it's the dead of winter in the north, here in the south, the seasons are reversed. Young emperor penguins are basking in the summer sunshine. They deserve it. They were born only five months ago, amid the most brutal conditions you can imagine.

Their eggs were kept warm by their fathers, who endured the long Antarctic winter hungry and alone. It was only when the chicks finally hatched that their mothers turned up with a warm welcome—their first meal.

Where could the females have possibly found food around here? In Antarctica there's only one place to do that. Just follow the young penguins as they head off for the sea....

King Penguins Swimming Underwater

Adélie Penguins Diving

Every summer Antarctica's shores brim with life!
And nobody enjoys the season more than Weddell
seals. All winter long they lived underwater, beneath
a thick ceiling of ice. They only returned to the surface
to breathe through the holes they made.

an you hold your breath for a minute? Seals can hold theirs for 20 minutes. How fast is your pulse? Their heart slows to 10 beats a minute, so they can save energy and stay under longer. Can you sleep underwater? Seals can!

The Weddell seal is not the only seal in Antarctica, but it lives farther south than any other mammal—or does it? Who's that steering a snow-mobile across the horizon?

Reclining Weddell Seal

Researcher Tracks
Whales in the Arctic

The polar regions draw explorers and scientists. They come on snowmobiles or dog sleds, aboard tiny planes or huge ships called icebreakers. They live in large research stations buried beneath the snow and in remote ice huts or tents. They're here to study the animal or plant life, astronomy, the weather—you name it! Or else they come simply for the adventure.

Dome of U.S. Antarctic Base

Arctic Dogsledding

Arctic Wolf

Step lightly as you leave now. There are places in the polar regions where your footprints might not go away for many years to come. That's how fragile this world is. The animals that live here may be tough, but they're also vulnerable. Even the cars we drive thousands of miles away can hurt them. The pollution from the exhaust is warming the Earth and beginning to melt the ice caps.

The sun is bidding its good-byes to the Arctic world. Through the long, cold months ahead, the animals will await its return.

A NOTE FROM THE NATIONAL GEOGRAPHIC SOCIETY

The Polar Regions

This map shows the northern and southern polar regions. White areas on the land represent permanent ice. White areas in the sea show the extent of winter sea ice.

Although at opposite ends of the globe, the polar regions are similar in many ways. Each is centered on one end of Earth's axis, the invisible line around which the planet rotates. Because the axis is tilted, each region has as much as six months of daylight and six months of darkness and experiences some of Earth's coldest temperatures. The Poles stay cold because even when they do get sun, the sun's rays are much weaker than at the Equator, and the vast polar ice fields reflect sunlight back into space, rather than absorbing it as the land does. Although about two-thirds of the Earth's fresh water is locked in polar ice caps, the regions are classified as deserts because they receive very little precipitation during the year.

But the two regions are as different as they are similar. The northern polar region is the area north of the Arctic Circle. Primarily an ocean covered by huge sheets of pack ice, it also includes parts of North America, Europe, and Asia. Except for Greenland, most of the land is ice-free in summer. By contrast, the southern polar region is a continent covered year-round by an ice sheet that averages more than a mile thick. Open seas separate it from neighboring landmasses.

Arctic and Antarctic wildlife are also quite different. The Arctic is home to many kinds of mammals, including polar bears, walruses, caribou, and wolves. These have long been hunted by Inuit and other Arctic peoples. In Antarctica, most wildlife lives in the surrounding seas or on some subantarctic islands. The largest native, year-round land animals are a few kinds of insects! Even penguins come ashore only to have their young. There has never been a permanent human population.

Many people are fascinated with the remote and beautiful polar regions. Both have been the target of some of the most adventuresome exploration in history. The National Geographic Society has been a supporter of such expeditions for more than a century and has reported on them in its publications.

Albatrosses on a Subantarctic Island

The polar regions are as fragile as they are harsh. They are becoming popular tourist destinations, and there is great risk that visitors will damage the environments they come to enjoy. The Antarctic Treaty, which is an agreement among 43 countries to preserve the continent for scientific research, has established guidelines for visitor behavior on that continent. Worldwide, there has been a growth in ecotourism: travel designed to protect and preserve wild places. As long as people are willing to be caretakers, the natural wonders of the polar regions will endure.

Antarctic Ecotourism Expedition

Inuit Camping in the Arctic

Published by the
National Geographic Society
1145 17th St. N.W.
Washington, D.C. 20036

John M. Fahey, Jr.
*President and Chief
Executive Officer*

Gilbert M. Grosvenor
Chairman of the Board

Nina D. Hoffman
Senior Vice President

William R. Gray
*Vice President and Director
of the Book Division*

Staff for this Book

Suzanne Patrick Fonda
Editor

Jennifer Emmett
Assistant Editor

Jonathan Grupper
Author

Marianne Koszorus
Art Director

Dorrit Green
Designer

Karen Gibbs
Illustrations Editor

Carl Mehler
Director of Maps

Vincent P. Ryan
Manufacturing Manager

Lewis R. Bassford
Production Manager

FRONT COVER: *A curious polar bear trots toward the camera on frozen land above the Arctic Circle.*

TITLE PAGE: *A young penguin trudges across icy Antarctica.*

Illustrations Credits

Cover, Kennan Ward; back cover, (top) Michio Hoshino/Minden Pictures, (bottom, both) Mitsuaki Iwago/Minden; endpapers, Jim Brandenburg/Minden; title page, Mitsuaki Iwago/Minden; pp. 2–3, Michio Hoshino/Minden; pp. 4–5, Kennan Ward; p. 4 and p. 6 (top and bottom), Flip Nicklin/Minden; p. 7, Jonathan Chester/Extreme Images; pp. 8–9, Flip Nicklin/Minden; p. 10 and p. 11 (top), Michio Hoshino/Minden; p. 11 (bottom), Gordon Wiltsie; pp. 12–13, Jim Brandenburg/Minden; p. 12, Wolfgang Kaehler; p. 13 (top) Kennan Ward; p. 13 (bottom) Wolfgang Kaehler; pp. 14–15, Michio Hoshino/Minden; p. 15, Kennan Ward; pp. 16 (both), Jim Brandenburg; pp. 16–17 and 17 (inset), Jim Brandenburg/Minden; pp. 18–19, Michio Hoshino/Minden; pp. 20–21, Des and Jen Bartlett; p. 20 (left), Michael Quinton/Minden, (right) Wolfgang Kaehler; p. 22 and p. 23 (top), Tui de Roy/Minden; p. 23 (bottom) and pp. 24–25, Mitsuaki Iwago/Minden; p. 25, Frans Lanting/Minden; pp. 26–27, Flip Nicklin/Minden; p. 27 (left), Galen Rowell; p. 27 (right) and pp. 28–29, Jim Brandenburg/Minden; p. 31 (top to bottom), Frans Lanting/Minden, Jonathan Chester/Extreme Images, Eugene Fisher; p. 32, Michio Hoshino/Minden.

To Kotchy, who is my north and south.

National Geographic would like to thank Kim Heacox, a former park ranger in Alaska's Glacier Bay, Denali, and Katmai National Parks, for reviewing the manuscript and illustrations and providing helpful comments.

Library of Congress
Cataloging-in-Publication Data
Grupper, Jonathan.
    Destination : polar regions / by Jonathan Grupper.   p. cm.
    Summary: Describes the unique environment of the world's polar regions and the plant and animal life that survives there.
    ISBN 0-7922-7143-2
    1. Zoology—Polar Regions—Juvenile literature.
[1. Polar Regions. 2. Zoology—Polar Regions. 3. Ecology—Polar Regions.]   I. Title.
QL104.G78   1999
590'.11—dc21   98-6413

A Polar Bear at Rest